PROJECT LEARNING USING DIGITAL PORTFOLIOS™

HOW TO CREATE DIGITAL PORTFOLIOS FOR COLLABORATIVE PROJECTS

AMIE JANE LEAVITT

Rosen
YA™

New York

Published in 2018 by The Rosen Publishing Group, Inc.
29 East 21st Street, New York, NY 10010

Copyright © 2018 by The Rosen Publishing Group, Inc.

First Edition

Library of Congress Cataloging-in-Publication Data

Names: Leavitt, Amie Jane, author.
Title: How to create digital portfolios for collaborative projects / Amie Jane Leavitt.
Description: New York, NY : Rosen Publishing, 2018. | Series: Project learning using digital portfolios | Includes bibliographical references and index. | Audience: Grades 7–12.
Identifiers: ISBN 9781508175247 (library bound book)
Subjects: LCSH: Electronic portfolios in education—Juvenile literature. | Digital media—Juvenile literature. | Education—Experimental methods.
Classification: LCC LB1029.P67 L43 2018 | DDC 371.39—dc23

Manufactured in China

CONTENTS

Since grade school, Adda has been dutifully collecting her most impressive accomplishments and archiving them inside a box that she stores under her bed. In this box, she tries to organize things as neatly as possible. She has a folder stuffed with stories she wrote in creative writing class. She has another folder brimming with her artwork, including countless ribbons she won in district contests. She has another folder with artifacts from her group projects, including photos, spiral-bound project details, and a page with links to videos her team uploaded to YouTube. She even has artifacts in her memory box that showcase her after-school and club activities.

Every once in a while, Adda pulls out the box to look through it or add something new. As a sophomore in high school, she does that now more frequently than ever before since she's involved in a variety of classes, projects, and organizations. After Adda files the materials into their appropriate slots, she slides the box back under her bed. She knows that unfortunately, someday, she'll probably just end up throwing out all of this stuff. After all, what good is a box of old papers anyway, especially if it's just stored under a bed for no one else to see and appreciate?

Adda's situation is not unique. She is like many other youth who have either collected these types of educational artifacts themselves or have parents who have collected them for them. They, too, feel frustrated that they have all of these great examples of achievement and growth but have nowhere to really display them. When it comes time to apply for college and jobs, these artifacts could help them get selected, but who is going to send in a whole box full of stuff to an admissions

Keeping your keepsakes in a box is great, but when it comes time to showcase your accomplishments, a digital portfolio is much more versatile.

committee or a hiring team? No one. The admissions committees and hiring teams would laugh at the absurdity of receiving such a collection.

Adda doesn't need to feel hopeless about her box of artifacts, and neither do any other youth who have done the same. The fact that she has collected these materials is a good thing. What Adda and other youth like her need to do is take advantage of the fact that they live in the digital age. There are tremendous storage and showcase opportunities available online. One of these is the digital portfolio. This platform lets people upload and organize their artifacts and then easily share the presentation with others.

Obviously, this idea of digital portfolios is new to Adda—after all, she'd already be storing her information that way if she had heard of it previously. When she first hears about it, she has many questions: What is a digital portfolio? How could it help me? What information is the most important to include? How can I make one?

If you also have these questions, then you're definitely in the right place. When learning about collaborative projects, you can go into great depth about digital portfolios and how to make them work for you in the future. Reading up on what collaborative projects are, and why they are important to include in a digital portfolio, can put you ahead of other students.

So let's get rolling into the wonderful world of digital platforms and collaborative learning.

CHAPTER ONE

WHAT IS A DIGITAL PORTFOLIO?

B y definition, a portfolio is a collection of works that illustrate a person's expertise, efforts, progress, creativity, knowledge, talents, abilities, leadership skills, and achievement. A curriculum vitae (similar in idea to a résumé) is a list of a person's accomplishments, education, skills, work history, and so forth. A portfolio is essentially a visual representation of the curriculum vitae. Instead of just saying that you can write code using a certain computer language as you would in a curriculum vitae, in a portfolio, you would actually include a sample of a program or website that you made using that specialized language.

SEEING IS BELIEVING

Portfolios have been used for decades by professionals seeking employment in their fields. Seeing is believing—and portfolios definitely allow a prospective employer or client to both see and believe in a professional's strengths and abilities. Generally, professionals bring their portfolio to a job interview or first meeting with a client to prove themselves and the kinds of work they are capable of performing.

For example, a photographer who wants to attract clients will make a collection of her photographs that shows the different styles she specializes in (landscapes, weddings, portraits, groups, and so forth). A journalist who wants to get hired by a local magazine publisher will include in his portfolio samples of both his published clips and unpublished articles and stories. A software engineer applying for jobs at an internet company will include in her portfolio examples of different types of web pages she has coded.

To many companies, portfolios are *the* most important piece of information that they look at. This is true for Jason Cranford

A digital portfolio is an essential component of successful job hunts in the 21st century. They allow applicants to showcase their talents, expertise, and skills in a visual and written format.

Teague, a senior creative director who views résumés from time to time. He explained in an article on Creativebloq.com that when he's hiring a person for his team, he doesn't care about what school a person went to, their GPA, the skills they "say" they have, or where they have been working recently—all things that would just be found on a standard résumé or curriculum vitae. "What I care about is *seeing* what you have done, i.e., your portfolio."

PRINTED PORTFOLIOS

The first portfolios used by professionals were printed on paper. They were organized using a variety of strategies, depending upon the size and subject matter of the works featured in the portfolio. For instance, a visual artist would oftentimes keep her portfolio in a large folder with handles and would carry it to interviews. She needed a large folder because the items in her folder were best viewed in their original size. On the other hand, other professionals would often use such organizing systems as a three-ring binder to consolidate their portfolios. An example of this includes a teacher looking for a job in the early 1990s. He would have made a portfolio showcasing examples of his lesson plans, teaching experience, leadership skills (in professional and community organizations), educational experiences, and personal hobbies. In the three-ring binder, he would have used tabbed dividers labeled with each of those category titles. In each section, he would have included such things as pictures of his students completing learning activities, samples of student work, and copies of lesson plans. His organization strategy would have helped him quickly show relevant examples to the hiring committee during an interview. Let's say they asked him the question, "What do you know about cooperative learning?" He could have

A QUARTET OF PORTFOLIO TYPES

Student portfolios are generally divided into four different types: process, showcase, hybrid, and assessment. People choose to use one type or another depending upon their purpose for making the portfolio.

Process. This type of portfolio shows the steps, or process, that students took to complete a project. It includes details on each stage of a project (beginning, middle, and end) and then includes reflection about each stage. Students tell what they learned in each part of the process and how they could improve it if they repeated it. This type of portfolio is also used as a "work-in-progress" portfolio because students can post projects they are working on (essay, poem, piece of artwork, computer program) and then go back and make alterations to it over time. The purpose of these portfolios is to give the students a chance to have dialogue about their work with family members, friends, and school faculty.

Assessment. The purpose of these portfolios is to show student competency and skill in certain areas. These types of portfolios are used to evaluate student performance at the end of a class instead of (or along with) traditional tests and quizzes. Teachers look at the material in assessment portfolios and see how the work measures up to the expectations for the project, and then issue a grade to the student for that work.

Showcase. For this type of portfolio, students choose to highlight their best work, skills, talents, and abilities. This type of portfolio is most similar to the employment, or career, portfolio that is used by professionals. With this type of portfolio, students include a selection of their best work across a variety of disciplines (classes). They often use a variety of media types in their portfolio, including blog posts, audio clips, picture collages, videos, images, and so forth.

Hybrid. The word "hybrid" means "a mixture of things." So, a hybrid portfolio is a combination of the above types of portfolios. It includes works in progress, the process the student went through to complete a project and his or her reflections, examples of the student's competencies and skills, and examples of the student's best work, skills, talents, and abilities.

responded, "Let me show you how I implemented that strategy in my classroom," and then shown pictures and lesson plans that backed up his explanation.

GOING DIGITAL

While printed portfolios definitely have their place and are still used by some professionals, many people today are opting to use the digital portfolio. The reasons for that are many. Here are five of them.

1. **No Longer Just on Paper.** Printed portfolios are limited to just things you can print on a piece of paper. Digital portfolios are not. They can include samples of work in a variety of formats including video, audio, interactive text, graphics, and programming, and a variety of sizes of images. When paper and digital are compared, digital definitely wins in versatility.

2. **Just Say No to Lugging Big Binders.** Professionals don't have to lug around a big folder or binder when they use digital portfolios. Everything fits neatly on the internet. Professionals just simply pull up their portfolio webpage on a mobile device or computer and showcase their top qualities to hiring committees and clients.

Digital portfolios allow for all kinds of media to be showcased including audio and video. These entries can include such options as interviews, songs, dance choreography, service projects, news reports, and theatrical performances.

3. **Greater Accessibility.** With a paper portfolio, the professional usually has to be in the room to showcase it. Not so
with a digital portfolio. A professionals can share the link to his
or her portfolios and then anyone who has the link can access
the person's samples. This allows professionals to reach a
greater, global audience. And of course the word "greater"
here is referring to the numerical size of the audience, not its
awesomeness.

4. **Saves Trees.** With a paper portfolio, professionals have to
manually print out samples to put into the binder or folder.
This, of course, means that more and more paper has to be
made by paper manufacturers, which ultimately impacts the
number of trees that are cut down. Therefore, going digital
definitely saves trees.

5. **Easily Updatable and Changeable.** Since so much
of what we do these days is done electronically, updating
a website with digital content is a fairly efficient and quick
process. The same is true with updating a digital portfolio. Video, photo, and text sharing is as simple as clicking a
button or two on a smartphone. When professionals need
to update their digital portfolios, they can use this sharing
technology to their advantage. With paper portfolios, the
content has to be located, printed, and then organized into
the binder. All of this takes a lot more time and effort than it
does with the digital process.

NOT JUST FOR PROFESSIONALS ANYMORE

Up until this point in this book, the discussion on portfolios has
been specifically on how they assist professionals as they seek
out employment and new clients. However, in today's world,
professionals aren't the only ones who are reaping the benefits

of portfolios, especially digital ones. Portfolios are now being used by students, beginning as early as preschool and extending through graduate school and post-grad years. Jag Vootkur, the CEO of KudosWall, explains in an article on LinkedIn, "Now, even middle schoolers are being asked to submit completed résumés to apply for summer programs. This is why an up to date, professional portfolio is now a necessity for students."

The world of education has discovered that digital portfolios are an excellent way to showcase student achievements and progress. Students find many benefits in building their own digital portfolios. Digital portfolios are used by students when they apply for college and internships, and they are a starting-off point for the eventual professional employment portfolio. This is one of the most critical ways that portfolios can help students in their lives. Yet, portfolios also have many other benefits, too. Here are some of them.

1. Establish Positive Digital Identities.

Since they're stored online, digital portfolios can be exhibited on PCs, laptops, tablets, and smart phones.

Portfolios are a way for students to use the internet as a showcase for achievement and positive behavior. It shows all of the great things that students have done over the course of their education, how they've learned and improved, and how they've served others and been good community members. Certainly, these examples will have long-term effects on the students as they enter their college and adult employment years.

2. **Provide Opportunities for Acquiring Digital Learning Skills.** Not only do the students get to establish an identity online, they get to learn how to do it. In this day and age, knowing how to use digital media is crucial for success in just about every avenue of life. Even our personal day-to-day inter-actions are impacted by technology. Students who have a very good understanding and expertise in this area will be that much more marketable and successful as adults.

3. **Show Progress Over Time.** Since portfolios can be started at the beginning of a person's education and can continue until graduation, they provide a way to show prog-ress over time. They also serve as a way to record all of the educational experiences that a student has, which serves as a type of storage facility. No longer do parents have to file away reports, pictures, and project notebooks in boxes in the attic.

Keeping portfolios in a digital format reduces the paper records that have to be kept.

All of these can be just stored on the student's online portfolio and will thereby take up zero physical space!

4. **Give Opportunities for Sharing and Collaboration.** An online portfolio allows students to share their ideas, projects, and other information with friends, family members, and teachers who can then discuss things with the student through a comments section. They can give suggestions for improvement and also just encouragement and a thumbs-up for a job well done. Portfolios can also be a way that students can work with other students on the same project. Those students can be in the same school, in the same state, or thousands of miles away in another country. The internet lets people of similar interests come together and work on a common goal together. Portfolios give students a way to complete those projects and also showcase them.

CHAPTER TWO

CONSTRUCTING A DIGITAL PORTFOLIO

There's no doubt that there are tremendous benefits of having a digital portfolio. When students hear about creating one, they're usually right on board! "That's really cool! I want to make one," they'll say. But then, they'll immediately ask, "How do I go about making one?"

CHOOSE A PLATFORM

The first step in making a digital portfolio is to choose a platform. There are many great digital portfolio platforms available, and many others will come into existence in

Portfolios can be created on formats such as WordPress. You can create a portfolio for a school project or a business.

the future. Some of the top picks are Google Drive Portfolios, Pathbrite, Bulb, Evernote, Weebly, WordPress, Seesaw, Kidblog, KudosWall, Easy Portfolio, Edublogs, LinkedIn, Three Ring, and VoiceThread. To find even more options, go to the search bar in your browser and search for the phrase "student digital portfolios" or a similar phrase bounded by quotation marks. Oftentimes, this search will result in a list of the platforms as well as articles that discuss the platforms. Articles are particularly helpful if they discuss the pros and cons of each platform. With that information, you can compare and contrast the platforms all in one place.

It might feel like a daunting task to choose a platform. Your first step in that process is to figure out what your goal is for your portfolio. Once you have that goal in mind, you can evaluate the platforms based on the following questions. You don't have to answer all of these questions, of course, just the ones that match your intent for your portfolio.

- Does the platform cost anything or is it free?
- What are the privacy settings? Can they be adjusted to limit or allow users depending upon the situation?
- What kinds of media (video, pictures, audio, text, and so forth) does the platform allow?
- What organizational tools does the platform have? Does it have tabs, columns, pages, and so forth to let you put different things in different places?
- Does the platform give you the chance to interact and collaborate with others? This can come in the form of comments sections on blogs and allowing multiple users to get on the same shared digital portfolio for group projects.
- Does the platform give ownership of the portfolio to the student? Meaning, if you were to move to another

school, could you take your portfolio with you? Or, once you graduate, are you allowed to take the portfolio with you?

- What design possibilities are there? Do all of the portfolios on the platform look the same (humdrum) or are there opportunities to show creativity in design?
- Can you access the platform only from a computer or will it also work on an iOS or Android device? Is it limited to only a mobile device? Note: it's best to have it available on all kinds of systems.
- Is there a space limit on the platform? Are students allowed to add only a certain amount of material to their portfolios? Or does the platform allow for unlimited storage space?

MATERIALS TO INCLUDE

Once you have chosen your platform, it is time to start figuring out what you want to put in your portfolio. Of course, once again, that all depends on your overall goal.

Let's say for example that college is your goal. What would you put on a college application portfolio? You'll want to have an area in the portfolio geared toward top educational projects that you've worked on during school, especially during your high school years. You'll want to have another area that shows leadership positions you've held or service opportunities you've participated in and an area that shows civic, work, club, or community involvement. If you have special talents and hobbies, those can also be included in a separate area as well. You'll want to have another area that shows collaborative projects that you've worked on with members of your

When you complete a group project of any kind, document it with videos, photos, and journal entries. These can then be included in a digital portfolio.

school, students in other states, and also students around the world. This last piece is particularly helpful since it shows that you have the ability to work with others in a team effort—a big component of many twenty-first century jobs.

Now, if your goal is something other than a college application portfolio, then of course you will have other materials you'll want to include. Maybe the purpose of the portfolio is to provide a place for members of a project to upload their materials, comment, interact, and share with others. If that is the goal, this portfolio will have a very different collection of content than a college-based one. And the type of platform you'd choose will be different as well.

Here are some other ideas of things you could include in a portfolio:

1. **Performance Art.** You could include a video of a play you were in, a storytelling performance, and so forth.
2. **Musical Performance.** You could include a video or audio of your performance on an instrument or vocally.
3. **Artwork.** Drawings, paintings, photography, graphic art, and photos of sculpture projects.
4. **Musical Composition.** For these you could include the printed sheet music or a video or audio of the music being performed.
5. **Writing.** Articles, stories, screenplays, poetry, essays, reports, and novels.
6. **Computer Games.** Games and programs you've designed and written.
7. **Websites.** Sites that you've designed on your own.
8. **Science, Engineering and Design.** You can include a video showcasing a robot you built, a Rube Goldberg contraption you designed, or a demonstration you did at a science fair.

HOW TO GET IT ALL ONLINE

Many of the platforms listed above have the capabilities of accepting videos, collages, and pictures directly from mobile devices. They also accept files that you've scanned or uploaded from a digital camera. Don't worry if you don't have access to this technology at home, because that doesn't eliminate your ability to make a digital portfolio. There are other places you can access these devices (computers, mobile

DO'S AND DON'TS OF A DIGITAL PORTFOLIO

There are many different ways to go about creating your digital portfolio. Some portfolios have information about the things you like or dislike. They can showcase your hobbies and achievements, too. When creating a portfolio online, always remember that parents, teachers, and future employers will see this. Here are some do's and don'ts to help show you what should appear in your digital portfolio.

Topics	Do's	Don'ts
Photos	Post a professional-looking photo of yourself. You may even consider posting a video introduction of yourself, too.	Don't use your portfolio like a photo-sharing or activity-sharing site and dump every single photo and video you've taken onto your portfolio. You need to be selective and share only the most appropriate and applicable media. You also want to make sure the things you share give a good, positive impression of who you are.
Content	Select examples in a variety of mediums (text, video, audio, slide presentations, and so forth) and in a variety of categories. This will show that you are a well-rounded individual.	Don't write pages and pages of text to describe a topic if a few sentences will do the trick. Remember, on the web brevity is the key! Don't think quantity beats quality, because it doesn't. While you want to show a variety of content, you don't want to overload and overwhelm your viewers with too much content. Be selective!

Presentation	Show your A-game immediately and throughout your site. Knock the socks off your viewers with everything you show them! Select only your most impressive accomplishments and feature them in a way that is visually pleasing.	Don't forget to organize, organize, organize. Ask people to take a look at your portfolio and give their impressions. Then use this data to improve the layout of your portfolio.

devices, video cameras, digital cameras, scanners). Many public libraries have this type of technology available for patrons to use. So do many public, private, and charter schools. Another place you can consider are makerspaces or FabLabs. These spaces specialize in up-to-date technology. Although this technology isn't always available for the general public to use, there are usually certain days when it is. Google "makerspaces" or "FabLabs" in your area and see what kinds of options are available to you. Give these organizations a call, explain your intent of building a digital portfolio, and they may have suggestions for you of other locations if their space isn't available for such purposes. Another way to access the technology you need is to network. Ask your teachers, principal, or guidance counselors if they have a suggestion of how you could access the technology for your portfolio. Generally, when students show a real interest and motivation to engage in educational projects, school faculty are eager to help.

Digital portfolios can allow for multiple users to enter content. This makes it a great way for groups to collaborate together and then record and showcase their efforts.

ORGANIZATION TIPS

Once your material is online, you need to develop an organization strategy for your portfolio. You can't just toss everything willy-nilly onto the home page and think it's going to look OK and be understandable to the people who visit your portfolio.

One obvious way to organize a showcase portfolio is to have different hyperlinked pages from a home page that take the viewer to different parts of your portfolio. On the homepage of a showcase-style portfolio, you'll want to have some information to describe who you are and why the viewer should visit the rest of your site. You can include such things as a professional-looking photograph of yourself, your own personal logo, a headline, a short personal statement that describes who you are and your intent for the portfolio, and contact information (controlled, of course, by the site's privacy settings). The hyperlinked pages can include such topics as science projects, collaboration, research essays, fiction and poetry, webpages, community involvement and service, computer programming and web design, robotics, engineering, honors and awards, public speaking, badges (certificates you've earned in online courses), courses, leadership, and references or testimonials.

CHAPTER THREE

WHAT'S A COLLABORATIVE PROJECT?

By definition, a collaborative project is one where two or more people work together to accomplish a specific goal. In school, students are often placed into groups to do a project. While this can be considered a collaborative project, it isn't necessarily. If only one or two people in the group do the work while the others in the group goof around, then the collaboration is not really effective. After all, according to the definition above, the members all need to work in order for it to be called a collaborative project. Every member of a collaborative group brings his or her own unique abilities and skills to the project and contributes in a meaningful way.

Collaboration is used all of the time in the modern business world. Let's look at the film industry for an example. When a movie is made, the actors aren't the only ones involved in the project. Other professionals also bring their expertise to the table, including set designers, writers, directors, and the camera crew. The film also needs experts in finance and advertising. Each one of these professionals works in a collaborative effort

Science projects and lab work that are completed either solo or with a group can be detailed from beginning to end on a digital platform.

to achieve a common goal, which is to finish a film within a set budget and get people to pay to watch it. Another example of collaboration in the workplace includes software development. While the software engineers might all have the same basic skills (they can write computer programs using certain computer languages), all kinds of tasks are needed to complete a finished project. For example, some engineers work on the front end of the software, or the stuff that the user sees. Other engineers work on the back end, or framework of the software that provides a foundation for the program. Some engineers develop programs to test the software for issues, or bugs. Another software engineer might work on developing security systems so that the software is protected. All of these tasks are essential to the success of the project and do not allow anyone a chance to "goof around" and not do his or her job. Collaboration is required in order for success.

Because these skills are necessary for the twenty-first-century workforce, students who participate in collaborative projects have advantages over those who do not. That's because while working on collaborative projects, students develop communication and negotiation skills, the ability to show respect for other people's knowledge and ideas, an appreciation that every member and position is valued and important, and the value of hard work and dedication to a job well done.

CLASSROOM COLLABORATION

One of the most basic types of collaboration takes place within the walls of a classroom. Each class—whether it be language arts, science, math, art, music, or social studies—provides opportunities for collaborative projects. For example, in a language arts class, three students may team up and practice their debating skills. One student takes a specific position on a topic, another student takes the opposite position, and the third student serves as the moderator. Then, the roles may be switched around for

Record any speeches or presentations you give. Then, include the best ones on your digital portfolio!

CONSTRUCTION TRADE CLASSES: THE ULTIMATE EXAMPLE OF CLASS COLLABORATION

A fabulous example of class-based collaborative learning takes place in high schools that offer construction trade classes. In these hands-on classes, students get to build an actual house (or other type of structure) from the ground up.

One example of this collaborative effort is found in a suburban area of Washington, DC, where students in a construction trade class built a house worth nearly one million dollars in 2016. During that school year, the students worked on most of the major aspects of the home's construction, including framing, flooring, installing drywall, and completing finish work and carpentry. As most students do in these construction trade classes, they left the plumbing and electricity to licensed contractors, as the law requires.

These collaborative classes help inspire students and give them rewarding real-world skills. Many, like Michael Powers from Lisle, Illinois, go on to work in the construction industry. In the comments section of a *Washington Post* article about the million-dollar house, Powers explained that in the 1970s he worked on several house-building projects in high school and after graduation went on to start his own company as a remodeling carpenter. He has now worked in that

(continuted on the next page)

(continued from the previous page)

capacity for more than thirty-five years. Other students may not choose to continue in the construction industry as Powers did, but they still carry these practical skills with them for the rest of their lives. Another commenter on the article stated that he is a lawyer nearing retirement but counts a collaborative experience of building a freestanding garage with a friend as one of the best experiences of his life.

another topic to give students a chance to practice each responsibility. Other examples of collaboration include students in a physics class building a Rube Goldberg machine and students in a computer class creating a game or website.

SCHOOL COLLABORATION

School-wide projects allow students to take collaboration to the next level. The possibilities of these school-wide interactions are only limited by the creativity of students and teachers.

A class-to-class collaboration is when two or more classes join together to work on a project. For example, a science class and a history class may work together on a field project where they gather information about pollution in a certain area and then compare it to data that has been gathered over a 100-year time period. They then look at the events in history that have caused the changes in the data, if there are any, or what things have stayed the same in the community to cause the similarities in the numbers. Another example of class-to-class collaboration would be an art class and a math class joining together to design and build a model of a bridge. The art students would contribute their expertise in advising what the bridge should look like and the math students would weigh in on whether or not those ideas would actually work based on real numbers and formulas.

An individual student collaboration is when individual students from a variety of classes work together to complete a project during a certain class period. Let's say a particular project is scheduled to be worked on during second period once a week. A student who has math during that period can sign up for the project and would be in charge of the math component. A student who is in science that period would bring his science expertise. A Spanish-language student would help ensure that the project had bilingual capabilities, while a history student would be in charge of any history-related issues. Students from other disciplines who signed up for the project (art, music, physical education, and so forth) would be in charge of making sure their respective areas were represented in the project. The students would either meet in person during that once-a-week schedule in a designated classroom or in the school library. Or they could stay in their classrooms and consult with each other through email, chat, or even video conferencing (if the computer was in a place where it wouldn't disturb the other students in the class, of course). As they work on their project throughout the semester, they would be held accountable for their work by showing their progress on a joint digital portfolio.

COLLABORATION HAS NO LIMITS

In the past, collaborative projects in businesses and schools were limited by geography because people needed to meet together in person in order to work on the projects. However, with the ability that people now have to communicate with others around the world through the internet, collaboration has no boundaries. Companies are able to place workers who do not live anywhere near each other on the same project or team. The team members communicate through video conferences, webinars, online chats, email, texts, FaceTime, and so forth. This has literally opened up a whole new world to companies because it allows them to utilize the skills and abilities of people from any background, culture, and location. Now, the best of the best, no matter who they are or where they are on the planet, can work together and create amazing products.

Schools have also discovered the same benefits of using the internet as a collaboration tool. Because of the internet, students in one part of the world are able to join with students in another part of the world to complete a joint project. They communi-

Digital platforms allow people to collaborate with others around the globe, just like this teen is doing through her laptop, microphone, and headset.

cate via Skype, email, and chat. They gather data and record it on the same platform so that everyone on the project can see it. They upload pictures, videos, and other evidence to show more details about their part of the project, too. These internet collaborations allow students to get real-world experience. They get to behave like real scientists, archaeologists, mathematicians, engineers, and historians as they work on problems and projects with people around the world.

In addition to thinking globally in terms of collaboration, schools have also thought locally. They have teamed up with businesses, lawmakers, professionals, and community members in their own areas to complete projects, too. Service learning is a prime example of this type of collaboration. With service learning, students complete a project that benefits a person in the community by garnering the assistance of members of the community. For example, students in the city of Wyoming, Michigan, worked with a contractor to build a wheelchair ramp at the home of a person in their community. The students applied the skills they had learned in school to measure, read blueprints, and construct the ramp. This collaborative effort required the ingenuity and hard work of everyone involved in order for it to be successful.

CHAPTER FOUR

COLLABORATIVE PROJECTS AND DIGITAL PORTFOLIOS

Digital portfolios and collaborative projects make great partners for two reasons. First, digital portfolios can provide the platform that members of the project can use to communicate, collaborate, and work on the project itself. Second, digital portfolios also provide a way for students who are applying for jobs or colleges to showcase some of their most impressive collaborative work across all subject areas and interests. This chapter will investigate both reasons in further detail.

PROVIDING A PLATFORM FOR COLLABORATION

Some digital portfolio platforms provide opportunities for participants in a project to all work together digitally. They can share information visually or through text. They can engage in conversations through chat and emails. There are many different types

Apps like Evernote can be used to help keep materials organized. With Evernote you can share your ideas with just about anyone!

of platforms that allow for collaboration. Here are descriptions of three of them.

- Google Drive allows collaborators to work on projects at the same time or at different times. One person, for example, could hop on the site and add content, data, or photos, and then when other users log on later, they can see it, comment on it, or revise it. If all of the members want to log on at the same time, they can use the platform to have a conversation about the project in real time.
- Evernote allows groups to set up project notebooks. Every member of the group can have access to the

THE WORLD IS OUR CLASSROOM

The goal of Skype in the Classroom is to empower students to become good global citizens and to play a part in solving some of the world's problems. Through this platform, students can take part in Skype lessons taught in real time by industry professionals or they can collaborate on projects with other students from around the world. They can sign up for virtual field trips where they get to tag along with an expert in such cool places as World War II bunkers in England, a mystery biome in Mount Rainier, a primate rescue center in the UK, a penguin breeding colony in Antarctica, or the top of Mount Everest! They can even invite guest speakers, like real authors, to their classrooms via Skype where they can listen to a lecture and then ask questions. Skype also provides a way for students to interact with penpals, or keypals as they're sometimes called. One teacher explained on Edutopia.org that her class connected with a class in Spain on Skype in the Classroom. They were in contact with each other throughout the year through letters and videos. Then, toward the end of the year, they set up a Skype session where the students could meet in real time.

Epals.com provides opportunities for students in grades pre-K through 12 to meet other students their age from around the world and also collaborate on projects together. One project featured on its website is called School Swap. In this program, schools are partnered with school in a different geographic location. They spend time getting to know each other—finding out what makes their school and country unique. Then, at the end of the project, each school makes a video about the *other* school that tells all about that school's best features.

Through the internet, the world has become a very small place where everyone can be interconnected.

notebook and add his or her own content to it. They can add things like photos, text, web clips, articles, data, and timelines of due dates.

- Conceptboard provides a way to organize all of the data that can be acquired during a project. The information is presented on idea boards. Members of the group can post items to the board (like a photo or image of a website), and then other members can comment on it. They can circle things they think need to be changed. They can add their approval for things they like. They can give status to what parts of the project are completed. Groups can create and share as many boards as they need to make for the project.

PROVIDING A SHOWCASE OPPORTUNITY

Simply put, including collaborative projects in a digital portfolio is, in one word, brilliant. As has been mentioned previously, the twenty-first-century workforce will only continue to be more collaborative-based as time goes on. Therefore, if you can illustrate in your portfolio that you already have the abilities to work together with others of all ages across disciplines, cultures, and geographical boundaries, then you are definitely going to be a cut above all of the other applicants vying for the same opportunities.

So, then, what are the best ways to showcase collaborative projects in a digital portfolio? The first is to include an area on the portfolio that is specifically set aside for collaborative projects so people who view your page can quickly find those experiences. The second way is to make sure that you include a variety of experiences that you've had in your classroom, school, community, and beyond. Include pictures or videos of the process and short, concise text to explain the pictures. Explain what your role was on the project. Take some time to reflect and tell what you learned from the project, what the pros and cons were about the project, and how you feel the project could be improved if repeated.

To get an idea of how to incorporate collaborative projects onto your digital portfolio ask a teacher or counselor for help. He or she can give you some ideas that you could implement

Theatrical performances, studio work, and film work make for great additions to a collaborative digital portfolio.

into your portfolio. You can also check to see what other students are doing by searching digital portfolios on the internet.

A film project could work well for someone who wants to work in film. Imagine you worked on the film project as a set designer. On your digital portfolio, you'll include all of the ways that you contributed to the project. You could embed a video interview "selfie" where you explain how you came up with the ideas for the set design and how you acquired the materials. You may want to post pictures of the design in different stages of completion with short summaries of the process. You can explain the ways you worked with the other members of the team to complete your part of the project. You can show the final product and give reflections on the overall experience.

A software engineering project could be great for someone who enjoys building apps or websites. For this project, let's say your role was as the front-end developer for website. On your digital portfolio, you'll describe how you worked with other members of the team to develop the website. You will want to explain the languages you used to write the code. You'll show clips of the website and even your various coding as examples. You could explain how you implemented changes suggested by the software tester and how you were able to work with the website designer to incorporate his or her ideas for the site.

A house-building project would be a great fit for someone who wants to flip houses. This could also be great for someone who is looking into going to school for architecture. Likely, if you worked on this project, you would have helped out in a variety of roles (framing, flooring, roofing, and so forth). You'd want to include photos of you completing the process or maybe even a video tour of the home in different stages of development. You could explain the

Construction work is generally a collaborative effort. Document such projects using video, interviews, journal entries, and photos. Then decide what components to include in your portfolio.

skills you learned on the job, how you felt about the experience, and what ideas you have for improvement on another similar project. This particular project would make a fantastic addition to a digital portfolio regardless of if you have interest in working in the construction industry or not. It shows that you are well rounded, are capable of working with a team to achieve a big goal, and are a hard worker who can learn a variety of skills.

A service-learning project could be great for a student who wants to be more involved. You could volunteer at a food bank or community center. Having a project like this to include on your digital portfolio allows you to show various positive characteristics about yourself: you are concerned about your community, want to do things for other people, are willing to donate your time and skills to help someone in need without getting paid, have the ability to learn new skills, and are willing to work with your peers and members of the community to make something happen. In a digital portfolio, you'd want to post a general summary of the project and whom (not a specific name or address) it benefited. You could also post a video interview at the site of the project where you explain your role in the project and what you learned in the process. You could include photos of the process, too. You could also explain what you learned by working with the other people on the project and how this collaborative effort was important for the project's success.

CHAPTER FIVE

LET'S COLLABORATE!

S ome students may not feel that they've had many opportunities for collaboration, and that could be you. Maybe your school doesn't offer these types of learning experiences. Or maybe you're homeschooled, so it's difficult to find other students to collaborate with. If you find yourself with those types of concerns, then just remember it's never too late. You can search out your own opportunities for collaborative learning so you will be able to include this type of project on your digital portfolio.

START YOUR OWN PROJECT

If you're interested in being part of a collaborative project, there's absolutely nothing stopping you from starting your own. This could either be an in-school venture or after-school experience.

If it's something that happens during school, of course you'll need to have the permission and support of the school administration. In order to do that, you'll need to compose a detailed plan for your project (goals, materials needed, people to be involved, time needed to accomplish, and so forth). Then, you'll have to "sell" the idea to your teacher or principal. This strategy is beneficial to you on many different levels. First, you find out what it's like to develop a project plan and discover everything that goes into it: brainstorming, researching, writing, and revising your ideas. Second, you discover what it takes to convince a person in authority to support a worthwhile idea. These experiences, in and of themselves, will be beneficial to you regardless of if the project idea is approved or not. If it isn't approved, you can still include the process you took to write the plan and pitch it on your digital portfolio—it will show your ingenuity and initiative. On the flip side, if your project is accepted (which of course, you hope it will be), you will have the opportunity to see a project through from inception to completion and will discover everything that goes along with that type of experience.

If you are homeschooled, you can also develop your own collaborative project. There's nothing that says you have to be enrolled in traditional school to be involved in these experiences. The idea-generation process will be the same for everyone regardless if they are in a homeschool or traditional school environment. However, for homeschoolers, it will be the gathering of other people to collaborate with that will likely be the most challenging. That's where homeschoolers need to think outside the walls of their own home! There are many types of people that can work together on a collaborative project, not just other kids in your same school. They can be people your own age, or they can be people of other ages. For example, children in elementary school could be included on a collaborative project. Or college students could be included, too. Trusted adults are also great people to collaborate with—they can be the parents of other homeschoolers, neighbors, religious leaders, club organizers, or your own aunts, uncles, and cousins. Another idea to

Brainstorming is a fabulous way to get ideas for collaborative projects. Get out of your normal environment—the new scenery can oftentimes bring forth a plethora of fresh ideas.

consider is that homeschoolers don't just have to include other homeschoolers in their project. If they hold their project's meeting times in the afternoons and evenings, then traditional school students can be included, too. See how this thought process opens up all new kinds of opportunities for you? A student in traditional school who wants to organize an afterschool collaborative project can also follow the same strategy mentioned for homeschoolers.

Now, regardless if you are homeschooled or in traditional school, you will want to make sure you have the support of a parent or guardian with your project. You won't likely need to write out a detailed project plan and present it to them in a formal way as was needed to pitch to a school administrator. However, you do need to give the parent or guardian enough thought-out details to show the purpose, plan, and structure of your project so he or she can feel comfortable with giving you the thumbs-up to proceed.

SEARCH AROUND ONLINE

There are hundreds of different collaborative projects available online for students to participate in with other students around the world. These projects range from those for young students (K–5) all the way through high school. Here are some examples:

1. **The Global Water Sampling Project.** This is a program for ages eleven through eighteen that is sponsored by the Center for Innovation in Engineering and Science Education (CIESE). It is a program where students from around the world collaborate on an environmental study program. Students collect samples of pond water in their local areas. They conduct water-sampling tests to determine pH level, nitrates, phosphates, coliform bacteria, and so forth. Then, they post their data on the project page and compare their findings with those of students from around the world. A similar project, Bucket Buddies is designed for students in grades 1–5. However, in that project, students identify the organisms in the samples, compare their findings with those of other areas, and look for relationships and trends in regard to geography, climate, and so forth.

2. **The Cultural Package Exchange.** iEARN, whose mission it to "learn with the world, not about the world," sponsors this program. With this particular project, students interact with other students in another country and culture. They exchange information about themselves in an online format at

the beginning. And then in a later stage of the program, they send via an international shipping service items from their own country and culture to share with their "sister" school. In the final stage, the students interact about the objects on the project forum and ask further questions for clarification about the items. So far, countries such as Algeria, Belarus, India, Mexico, Morocco, Thailand, the United States, and Singapore (among at least ten others) have participated in the project.

3. **RainForest ArtLink.** It is a project sponsored by Creative Connections, an international cultural education organization. In this project, students from countries around the world team up with a school in the American rain forest (either Guatemala, Costa Rica, or Brazil). The classes interact with each other in real time through video conferencing and share art (visual and performing) with each other. For example, the classes could paint or draw pictures showing something important in their environment or culture or they could share a dance or musical number, too. The program allows students to reinforce what they are learning in social studies, writing, oral and written pre-sentation skills, art, and foreign languages. One student who participated in a program through Creative Connections said on in YouTube video, "It opens your eyes to what life is like in other places around the world, even if you don't have the opportunity of visiting those places."

JOIN CLUBS

Clubs are a great way for students to engage in collaborative projects. There are clubs dedicated to particular subject matter (like engineering and science clubs) and also those dedicated to particular groups of people (boys only and girls only clubs, religious-themed clubs, and so forth). To find a club in your area, you can conduct a simple search online with a phrase that matches your interest. For example, if you wanted to find a club for engineering in your area, you could type "engineering

Work on tech projects with others and document your efforts. Then include photos and videos of the process in a digital portfolio.

youth clubs," and see what results come up. You can narrow your search by including your town's name. However, it's better to stick to a larger search at the beginning and then look at the individual clubs to see if they have a branch in your area. If you

don't have a particular preference on the type of club and just want to find examples of all youth clubs in your area, search using a phrase such as "youth organizations" or "youth clubs." Then, look into the ones that sound interesting to see if there are options in your particular town or city.

VOLUNTEER WITH RELIGIOUS, COMMUNITY, CIVIC, OR SERVICE GROUPS

Many religious, community, and civic groups provide opportunities for young people to join together on weeknights or weekends and participate in collaborative activities. Milbrey McLaughlin wrote about community groups in an article published by Stanford's John W. Gardner Center for Youth and Their Communities. She said that community groups provide young people a chance to gain closer associations with peers by engaging in positive activities that benefit society. Some of these include service projects (like adopting a highway), team-building activities, and the raising of funds or goods for worthy causes (like donating blankets to a homeless shelter). To find these groups, conduct online searches for "religious youth groups near me" or "youth groups near me."

YOUTH ORGANIZATIONS AND SERVICE OPPORTUNITIES

This chart shows some examples of clubs and organizations that youth can join and also organizations that offer service opportunities to both youth and adults. If you'd like to find out more about these organizations, visit their websites. Remember, this is just a short list. There are many other organizations that can be found by conducting an online search.

Youth Organizations and Clubs	Organizations That Offer Service Opportunities
Boy Scouts of America	Youth Service Opportunity Project (YSOP)
Girl Scouts	Volunteer Match
4-H	Network for Good
Lions Quest	America's Promise
Camp Fire	Points of Light Foundation & Volunteer Center
Boys and Girls Clubs	SERVEnet
Federation of Galaxy Explorers	American Red Cross
YMCA	United Way
Girls for a Change	Salvation Army
Junior States of America	Habitat for Humanity
Federation of North American Explorers—Canada	Dosomething.org
FFA	Operation Gratitude
National Junior Horticultural Association	
Students Today, Leaders Forever	

CHECK OUT LOCAL COLLEGES, UNIVERSITIES, AND MUSEUMS

Local institutions of higher education generally offer a variety of educational opportunities for youth. A quick Google search of the phrase "universities youth programs" generated nearly fifty-one million results. There are programs at such locations as Johns Hopkins, Western Washington University, University of Utah, Northwestern University, Auburn University, Purdue, California Academy of Sciences, and Stanford to name just a few. These programs are held both during the summer and during the school year and range from camps, classes, and workshops. Many include collaborative projects and activities. Conduct a similar search online to find programs at colleges, universities, and museums in your area.

CONSIDER MAKERSPACES, FABLABS, AND HACKATHONS

Makerspaces and FabLabs are terrific places to look for collaborative opportunities. These spaces provide opportunities for people to make things and collaborate with others while doing so. These fabrication laboratories are generally filled with all kinds of machinery and high-tech equipment. They allow people to make robots, woodworking projects, computer programs, and even 3-D printed clothing. The main emphasis of these places is the idea of community. People can make these things on their own if they have the equipment, but in makerspaces and FabLabs they are encouraged to collaborate with others, even if it's just to ask for advice or suggestions on how to make a project better.

If you like technology-related projects, then sign up for a hackathon! These are fantastic ways to collaborate with other like-minded people and create innovative projects in a work-filled weekend.

Hackathons are events where people interested in technology come together to create new products from the ground up. They join together in randomly selected teams and work for twenty-four to thirty-six hours (usually without sleeping) in the race to the finish. At the end of the event, the teams present their products and vie for prizes. The experiences that people attain by participating in hackathons are extremely beneficial and definitely worthy of finding a place in a digital portfolio.

PERFECT MATCH

One of the points of having a digital portfolio is to showcase how you've grown and developed over your educational experience. Including collaborative projects in a digital portfolio shows a crucial element of that growth: being able to work effectively together with others to achieve a common goal. The more you can show your ability to do this in a digital portfolio, the more marketable you will be in the college and career world. The bottom line is this: none of us are alone on this planet, thankfully. And we need the great ideas and contributions of everyone in order for the planet to thrive. Collaborative projects allow people to cross age, cultural, language, and geographic boundaries to develop deeper understanding and appreciation for what everyone has to offer.

GLOSSARY

assessment Evaluation or testing.

blueprint A design or plan for a model or other structure that is written out as a technical drawing.

carpenter A person who works with wood; also called a woodworker.

collaborate To work with or cooperate with others to achieve a common goal.

cooperative learning A learning style that encourages students to work together in groups or with partners.

curriculum vitae A list of a person's accomplishments, education, skills, work history, and so forth; it is generally much more extensive than a résumé.

drywall A type of board that is often used in constructing the inside walls and ceilings of various buildings and is made up of plaster, wood pulp, and other materials.

framing Making the framework of a house, usually out of such materials as wood or steel.

globally On a worldwide scale.

hackathon An event that lasts a specific amount of time, generally one or two days or over a weekend, where computer engineers come together and create new software or hardware from the ground up.

hybrid A mixture of things.

keypals People who write back and forth to each other using a computer (keyboard) and send the letters electronically through the internet. Also called e-pals or e-penpals.

makerspace A place where people gather to create, invent, and learn as a member of an innovative community. These spaces often have state-of-the-art technology (3-D printers, software, electronics, and so forth) that allow people to create. They can also offer woodworking tools, sewing machines, and other equipment that is not digital in nature.

penpals People who write back and forth to each other through letters that are sent through the mail.

platform When it applies to computers, it is hardware or software that is used to provide a particular service.

portfolio A collection of works that illustrate a person's expertise, efforts, progress, creativity, knowledge, talents, abilities, leadership skills, and achievement.

résumé A brief listing of a person's achievements, education, and skills that generally doesn't go past two pages in length.

Rube Goldberg A term, when used as an adjective, that describes a contraption or a machine that solves a simple task in an overly complicated way. The expression is named after the American cartoonist and inventor Rube Goldberg, who lived from 1883–1970.

video conferencing Communication that happens between two or more people using video cameras and an internet connection and allows face-to-face discussions to happen when people are unable to meet in person.

FOR MORE INFORMATION

American Councils for International Education
1828 L Street NW, Suite 1200
Washington, DC 20036
(202) 833-7522
Website: http://www.americancouncils.org
This international nonprofit is dedicated to providing access to
educational opportunities for people around the world. It was
started in 1974 as a way for help promote exchange between
scholars in the United States and scholars on the other side of
the Iron Curtain (the Soviet Union). Its success in its early efforts
paved the way for collaboration in curriculum, assessment, and
innovation in 80+ countries around the world today.

Canadian Scholarship Trust Plan (CST)
Inspired Minds Learning Project
1600-2235 Sheppard Avenue
East Toronto, ON M2J 5B8
Canada
Website: http://www.learningproject.cst.org
This organization provides an innovative vision of a "Canada of
the Future," for children up to age seventeen. Organizations,
institutions, and communities are invited to participate in the
Inspired Minds Learning Project by submitting ideas for both
big and large projects that will help Canadian children "grow,
learn, and develop."

iEARN (International Education and Resource Network)
USA Branch
475 Riverside Drive, Suite 450
New York, NY 10115

(212) 870-2693

Website: https://www.iearn.org, http://www.us.iearn.org

iEARN (which is an acronym for International Education and Resource Network) is the world's largest nonprofit global network. There are iEARN organizations in 140 countries around the world reaching more than 30,000 schools and youth organizations and 2 million students every year. The purpose of the organization is to help students "learn with the world, not just about it." This is accomplished through collaborative projects that are designed to answer the overarching question, "How will this project improve the quality of life on the planet?"

Kidlink Association

c/o Stellan Kinberg

Lotta Svärdsgata 4C

SE-41504 Göteborg

Sweden

Website: http://www.kidlink.org

The purpose of Kidlink is to "promote global dialogue among the youth of the world" through the use of (primarily) electronic communications. Projects listed on the site are suggested and monitored by global volunteers. The organization has been offering these services to youth around the world for free since 1990.

National Association of Independent Schools (NAIS)

1129 20th Street NW, Suite 800

Washington, DC 20036

(202) 973-9700

Website: http://www.nais.org

NAIS is a nonprofit association for independent nonprofit private schools. Its goal is to provide services for these school (and the student who go there) through excellence, equity, efficiency, and emotion. Resources on all topics, including project-based learning, are available through the website and related publications (*Independent Teacher* magazine).

Taking It Global (TIG)
117 Peter Street, Suite 212
Toronto, ON M5V 0M3
Canada
(416) 977-9363
Website: http://www.tigweb.org
Taking It Global is dedicated to connecting students around the world and giving them an avenue to build teams and collaborate on important projects that have positive impact on a global scale. Its programs span such topics as global education, social innovation, and digital youth engagement.

WEBSITES

Because of the changing nature of internet links, Rosen Publishing has developed an online list of websites related to the subject of this book. This site is updated regularly. Please use this link to access the list:

http://www.rosenlinks.com/PROJL/collaborate

FOR FURTHER READING

Bender, Diane. *Design Portfolios: Moving from Traditional to Digital.* New York, NY: Fairchild Books, 2012.

Cameron, Schyrlet, and Carolyn Craig. *Project-Based Learning Tasks for Common Core State Standards, Grades 6–8.* Greensboro, NC: Mark Twain Media, 2014.

Conzemius, Anne E., and Jan O'Neill. *The Handbook for Smart School Teams.* Bloomington, IN: Solution Tree Press, 2014.

Krauss, Jane, and Suzanne K. Boss. *Thinking Through Project-Based Learning: Guiding Deeper Inquiry.* Thousand Oaks, CA: Corwin, 2013.

Larmer, John, John Mergendoller, and Suzie Boss. *Setting the Standard for Project-Based Learning: A Proven Approach to Rigorous Classroom Instruction.* Alexandria, VA: ASCD, 2015.

Laur, Dayna. *Authentic Learning Experiences: A Real World Approach to Project-Based Learning.* New York, NY: Routledge, 2013.

Light, Tracy Penny, Helen L. Chen, and John C. Ittelson. *Documenting Learning with ePortfolios: A Guide for College Instructors.* San Francisco, CA: John Wiley & Sons, 2012.

McGuinness, Eamonn. *Collaborative Project Management: A Handbook.* Boston, MA: BrightWork Publications, 2016.

Madden, Dr. Therese M. *Creating Your Electronic Portfolio: Envisioning and Creating an Electronic Portfolio.* CreateSpace Independent Publishing Platform, 2015.

Renwick, Matt. *Digital Student Portfolios: A Whole School Approach to Connected Learning and Continuous Assessment.* Virginia Beach, VA: Powerful Learning Press, 2015.

Wolpert-Gawron, Heather. *DIY Project Based Learning for ELA and History.* New York, NY: Routledge, 2016.

BIBLIOGRAPHY

Balingit, Moriah, and Donna S. George. "This House—Built with the Help of High School Students—Is on the Market for $935,000," *Washington Post*, June 12, 2016. https://www.washingtonpost.com/local/education/this-house--built-with-the-help-of-high-school-students--is-on-the-market-for-935000/2016/06/12/f28c7646-1c92-11e6-b6e0-c53b7ef63b45_story.html.

Carlisle, Jennifer. "3 Ways Digital Portfolios Benefit Your Students." The Art of Education, November 2015. https://www.theartofed.com/2015/11/04/3-ways-digital-portfolios-benefit-your-students.

CMC Education. "Community House Ramp Documentary." YouTube, June 11, 2013. https://www.youtube.com/watch?v=EdFFMBfnXHg.

Creativebloq.com. "5 Things Your Portfolio Should Have." June 4, 2015. http://www.creativebloq.com/portfolios/5-things-i-want-see-your-portfolio-61515105.

CreativeConnections. "Creative Connections: My 21st Century Learning Experience." YouTube, April 16, 2015. https://www.youtube.com/watch?v=jvCZA8C7Nmk.

Elmore, Kal. "Planning a Portfolio for Your College Application." CollegeBasics.com. Retrieved October 10, 2016. http://www.collegebasics.com/planning-for-college/your-high-school-path/156-planning-a-portfolio-for-your-college-application.html.

GDC Team. "How to Use LinkedIn and Evernote for Building Student Portfolios." Global Digital Citizen Foundation. Retrieved October 8, 2016. https://globaldigitalcitizen.org/how-to-use-linkedin-and-evernote-for-building-student-portfolios.

Hicks, Kristen. "5 Free Tools for Making Digital Portfolios."
    Edudemic.com, February 9, 2015. http://www.edudemic
    .com/tools-for-digital-portfolios.
Holland, Beth. "Digital Portfolios: The Art of Reflection." Eduto-
    pia, June 30, 2015. http://www.edutopia.org/blog/digital
    -portfolios-art-of-reflection-beth-holland.
McLaughlin, Milbrey. "Community Counts: How Youth Organiza-
    tions Matter for Youth Development." John W. Gardner Center
    for Youth and Their Communities. Stanford Graduate School
    of Education, April 2000. https://gardnercenter.stanford.edu
    /publications/community-counts-how-youth-organizations
    -matter-youth-development.
Mim, Lisa. "Pen Pals in the 21st Century." Edutopia.org, Novem-
    ber 2, 2013. http://www.edutopia.org/blog/pen-pals-in-21st
    -century-lisa-mims.
OwnYourOwnFuture.com. "Building a College Portfolio, Prep,
    Grades 7–9." Retrieved October 11, 2016. http://www
    .ownyourownfuture.com/files/documents/building-a-college
    -portfolio-e.pdf.
Regis University Electronic Portfolio Project. "e-Portfolio Basics:
    Types of e-portfolios." Retrieved October 9, 2016. http://
    academic.regis.edu/laap/eportfolio/basics_types.htm.
Strang, Tami. "Three Reasons ePortfolios Matter to Today's
    College Students." Cengage Learning, April 29, 2015. http://
    blog.cengage.com/three-reasons-eportfolios-matter-to
    -todays-college-students.
Vootkur, Jag. "A Beginner's Guide to Student Portfolios."
    LinkedIn, August 22, 2016. https://www.linkedin.com/pulse
    /beginners-guide-student-portfolios-jag-vootkur.

INDEX

ABOUT THE AUTHOR

Amie Jane Leavitt graduated from Brigham Young University and is an accomplished author, researcher, and photographer. She has written numerous books for children and young adults, has contributed to online and print media, and has worked as a consultant, writer, and editor for numerous educational publishing and assessment companies. To check out a listing of Ms. Leavitt's current projects and published works, check out her website at www.amiejaneleavitt.com.

PHOTO CREDITS

Cover wavebreakmedia/Shutterstock.com; p. 5 Sharon Foelz/ E+/Getty Images; © iStockphoto.com/Geber86; pp. 12, 24 Rawpixel.com/Shutterstock.com; p. 14 © iStockphoto.com/ Hocus Focus Studio; p. 15 PeopleImages/DigitalVision/Getty Images; p. 17 David M G/Shutterstock.com; p. 20 michaeljung/ Shutterstock.com; p. 27 Lucky Business/Shutterstock.com; p. 28 Hill Street Studios/Blend Images/Getty Images; p. 32 Dragon Images/Shutterstock.com; p. 35 dennizn/Shutterstock.com; p. 37 sdecoret/Shutterstock.com; p. 39 Fabio Pagani/Shutterstock .com; pp. 40–41 Lisa F. Young/Shutterstock.com; p. 45 Christopher Edwin Nuzzaco/Shutterstock.com; pp. 48–49 DGLimages/ Shutterstock.com; p. 52 Bloomberg/Getty Images; back cover Alexandr III/Shutterstock.com; interior pages graphic pp. 7, 17, 26, 34 Ron Dale/Shutterstock.com.

Designer: Michael Moy
Editor and Photo Researcher: Ellina Litmanovich